EXPLORING CIVIL

THE RISE

1972

SELENE CASTROVILLA

Franklin Watts®
An imprint of Scholastic Inc.

Content Consultant

A special thank you to Ryan M. Jones at the
National Civil Rights Museum for his expert consultation.

Library of Congress Cataloging-in-Publication Data
Names: Castrovilla, Selene, 1966– author.
Title: The rise: 1972 / Selene Castrovilla.
Other titles: Exploring civil rights.
Description: First edition. | New York : Franklin Watts, an imprint of
  Scholastic Inc., 2023. | Series: Exploring civil rights | Includes
  bibliographical references and index. | Audience: Ages 10–14. |
  Audience: Grades 7–9. | Summary: "Series continuation. Narrative
  nonfiction, key events of the Civil Rights Movement in the years after
  1965. Photographs throughout"—Provided by publisher.
Identifiers: LCCN 2022039920 (print) | LCCN 2022039921 (ebook) |
  ISBN 9781338837629 (library binding) | ISBN 9781338837636 (paperback) |
  ISBN 9781338837643 (ebk)
Subjects: LCSH: African Americans—Civil rights—History—20th
  century—Juvenile literature. | Civil rights movements—United
  States—History—20th century—Juvenile literature. | Civil rights
  workers—United States—Juvenile literature. | BISAC: JUVENILE
  NONFICTION / Social Topics / Civil & Human Rights | JUVENILE NONFICTION
  / History / General
Classification: LCC E185.615 .C357 2023 (print) | LCC E185.615 (ebook) |
  DDC 323.1196/073—dc23/eng/20220823
LC record available at https://lccn.loc.gov/2022039920
LC ebook record available at https://lccn.loc.gov/2022039921

10 9 8 7 6 5 4 3 2 1   23 24 25 26 27

Printed in China   62
First edition, 2023

Composition by Kay Petronio

COVER & TITLE PAGE:
U.S. Congresswoman Shirley Chisholm
announces her candidacy for the
Democratic Party's presidential
nomination on January 25, 1972.

The Way It Was

The year 1865 was an important one in U.S. history. The American Civil War (1861–1865) ended and the Thirteenth **Amendment** to the U.S. Constitution was passed, **abolishing** slavery. This period of time also introduced Black codes in the form of **Jim Crow** laws. These laws restricted where people of color could live and work and were especially strict in the American South.

Jim Crow laws enforced **segregation**. Under the racial policy of "separate but equal," Black Americans could be given access to separate facilities if their quality was equal to that of white facilities. In reality, however, there was no equality. African Americans were forced to attend separate and inadequate schools and live in run-down neighborhoods.

The Fight Begins

As Jim Crow practices continued, two prominent **civil rights** organizations emerged. The National Association of Colored Women's Clubs (NACWC) was founded in 1896 by a group of politically active women, including Harriet Tubman. Members of the association dedicated themselves to fighting for voting rights and for ending racial violence in the form of **lynchings** against African Americans.

The National Association for the Advancement of Colored People (NAACP), founded in 1909, followed in the NACWC's footsteps. The NAACP focused on opposing segregation and Jim Crow policies. Both organizations would be crucial in the coming fight for justice.

Lasting Changes

In the following years, the Great Depression (1929–1939) and World War II (1939–1945) left Black Americans fighting for their lives at home and overseas. The 1954 U.S. Supreme Court decision in the *Brown v. Board of Education of Topeka* case challenging school segregation finally put an end to "separate but equal" in public schools. The years between 1955 and 1965 would serve as the heart of the civil rights movement. Rosa Parks refused to give up her seat on a bus, sparking the Montgomery bus **boycott**. The Reverend Dr. Martin Luther King, Jr., emerged as a leader and organized the March on Washington for Jobs and Freedom, the largest civil rights demonstration at the time.

The 1960s and 1970s further ignited those yearning for equal opportunities under the law. **Activists** continued to persevere, resulting in lasting changes for the African American community.

1972

In this book, read about the state of American civil rights in 1972 and learn about the push for diverse voices in government. The year marked the candidacy of the first Black person, also a woman, to run for president of the United States. The Equal Rights Amendment would finally make it through Congress, after first being introduced in 1923. **Indigenous** Americans who had long suffered **prejudice** and great loss at the hands of the **federal** government would set off on a journey to Washington and demand their rights. The Vietnam War continued to take thousands of young American lives—a large amount of them African American. President Nixon's plans for further involvement would ignite new protests around the country. The year 1972 would see more American minorities carve a path toward fairness and equal representation in the government, which is still being traveled today. ■

The National Black Political Convention (NBPC) in March 1972 brings approximately 8,000 people together.

CHISHOLM FOR PRESIDENT

Shirley Chisholm opens her presidential campaign with a rally at the Cambridge Community Center in Cambridge, Massachusetts, on February 15, 1972.

1

Unbought and Unbossed

Congresswoman Shirley Chisholm announced her candidacy for the Democratic Party's presidential nomination on January 25, 1972. She became the first African American to run for a major party's nomination for president of the United States. She also became the first woman to run for the Democratic Party's presidential nomination.

Chisholm made her announcement inside the auditorium of the Concord Baptist Church elementary school in the Bedford-Stuyvesant neighborhood in Brooklyn, New York. The 47-year-old representative stated that she was not the candidate of Black America, though she was Black and proud, and she was not the candidate of the country's women's movement, though she was equally proud of that. She was the candidate of the people. Her slogan was "Unbought and Unbossed," meaning that she was fighting for working people, not just for the wealthy people who contributed to her campaign.

Beginnings

Shirley Chisholm's parents were working-class immigrants from Guyana and Barbados. Her father worked in a burlap bag factory and as a baker. Her mother was a seamstress and a **domestic** worker. Raising children while working became a challenge for her parents, who sent five-year-old Shirley and her two sisters to live with their grandmother in Barbados. Chisholm later credited her grandmother for teaching her that she mattered and for providing her with a wonderful education. She returned to the United States at age 10 to live with her parents, but always thought of herself as a Barbadian American. She eventually became a teacher, one of the only career options she saw for a woman.

In 1953, Chisholm entered politics when she volunteered to work for the campaign of Lewis S. Flagg, Jr., a man seeking to be the first Black judge in Brooklyn. The campaign was organized by Wesley McDonald Holder, an African American staffer in the Brooklyn district attorney's office. He decided to organize the campaigns of Black candidates. Flagg won, and Chisholm continued working with Holder on African

Chisholm is sworn in as the first African American woman to serve in the House of Representatives on January 3, 1969.

American candidates' campaigns in a group called the Bedford-Stuyvesant Political League (BSPL). In 1958, she left the group after clashing with Holder over his refusal to allow women members of the group to have more decision-making power. However, 10 years later, Holder ran Chisholm's campaign for the House of Representatives. She became the first Black woman elected to Congress. Chisholm only hired women for her staff, and half of them were Black.

Freedom's Price

Being "unbought and unbossed" meant that Chisholm didn't owe any political favors in return for campaign donations. She didn't have to answer to big-money contributors who would expect her to promote their interests instead of hers if she was elected. But freedom came with a price. Chisholm faced the challenge of running a low-budget campaign, with just $44,000 in contributions raised at the time of her announcement and the expectation of raising $300,000 more at upcoming fundraising events. Most Democratic candidates spent at least $1 million. But her bigger challenge was overcoming the double prejudice she faced. She said that being a woman was a bigger hurdle than being Black. Men had a hard time considering a woman as an equal.

She did not have the support of most Black men, either. She said that Black men felt she was trying to take power from them. Black men must step forward, she stated, but that did not mean that

Chisholm flashes the "victory" sign in her Brooklyn, New York, presidential campaign headquarters.

Chisholm (seated center, right) and her fellow founding members of the Congressional Black Caucus.

Black women must step back. Of the 13 members of the Congressional Black Caucus, of which she was a founding member, only five men supported her. And only two of them were vocal about it. Her former campaign manager, Wesley McDonald Holder, did not support her, either.

Chisholm also could not get the National Women's Political Caucus (NWPC) to support her, even though she had been one of its founders the previous year. This organization was dedicated to increasing women's participation in politics.

Paving the Way

While the other Democratic candidates expressed confidence in victory, Chisholm admitted she did not think she would win the election—but she was determined to pave the way for people of ethnic groups in the future, including African Americans, who could perhaps win the office. She hoped to win enough **delegates** to the Democratic National Convention in July that she could influence decisions within the party and help create the party's platform—its declaration of where it stood on issues.

Chisholm felt strongly about certain issues and hoped that people would listen to her if she was running for president. She declared that she was running an issue-driven campaign, promising to bring needed change in America. Ending the war in Vietnam was Chisholm's primary concern. Seventy-five percent of the federal budget was being spent on continuing what she called an "immoral war."

U.S. soldiers in Vietnam rush to carry their wounded comrade to a helicopter.

Anti-Apartheid Bill

In February, Representative Ronald V. Dellums of California introduced the Congressional Black Caucus's first bill concerning **apartheid** into Congress. Apartheid, meaning separateness, was a South African system of **discrimination** and segregation because of race. Black South Africans were **economically**, socially, and politically **oppressed** by the country's white minority.

It would take 14 years of persistence and more than 15 bills concerning apartheid, but Dellums and others succeeded in getting a bill passed in 1986. The bill ended all U.S. financial dealings with South Africa, including business conducted by American corporations, until they ended apartheid. It was called the Comprehensive Anti-Apartheid Act of 1986.

Ronald V. Dellums made history as the first African American to serve on and chair the House Armed Services Committee.

A Stark Difference

Defeating President Richard M. Nixon was certainly the endgame, but there were eight other white men who were Chisholm's opponents in the race for the Democratic nomination. George Wallace's belief system was the most strikingly different from hers. The former governor of Alabama had been known as the face of southern segregation. But Wallace and Chisholm did have something in common. He, too, refused to be bought by corporations and wealthy donors, and he also criticized the government for not listening to the people.

They were both outsiders, standing on opposite ends politically, while the heavily funded candidates got more serious attention. Campaigning in Florida, Wallace told voters that if they couldn't support him in the primary, rather than vote for the candidates who were in the spotlight, they should vote for Chisholm. This association hurt Chisholm since her supporters

President Richard Nixon and his wife, Pat, greet crowds from the doorway of Air Force One during his 1972 campaign for reelection.

were opposed to Wallace's beliefs. Voters felt Chisholm might be in a **conspiracy** with Wallace for votes. She came in seventh in the number of delegate votes in Florida, where she thought she would do well.

Angela Is Freed

Angela Davis, a Black **Communist** activist and university assistant professor, had been arrested on murder charges in New York City on October 13, 1970. She had not killed anyone, but guns she owned had been used in the armed takeover of a courtroom in Marin County, California, which led to the deaths of four people, including Judge Harold Haley. Davis was acquainted with one of the people on trial the day the takeover occurred.

The "Free Angela" movement had been swelling across America for nearly a year and a half. Many Americans felt Davis should not have been charged with a crime. Rodger McAfee, a dairy farmer from Fresno, California, paid Angela Davis's $102,000 bail on February 23, 1972—five days before her trial. Steve Sparacino, a wealthy business owner, also contributed. Some of her legal expenses were paid by the United Presbyterian Church, which contributed $10,000 to the Angela Davis Legal Defense Fund.

Where We At

From January 2 to January 20, 1972, a group of Black women artists called Where We At (WWA) presented an exhibit called the Cookin' & Smokin' exhibition in Harlem, New York City. WWA gave African American women artists a space and community of their own. They were often overshadowed by Black male artists and white female artists. Through WWA, Black female artists could practice and showcase their talents, as well as share resources and concerns. Many of these women did not consider themselves professional artists because they had been conditioned to think they were not capable. WWA provided them with the courage to believe in themselves and pursue their art.

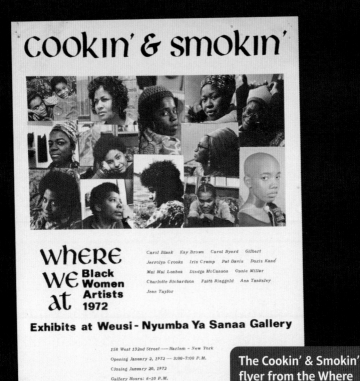

The Cookin' & Smokin' flyer from the Where We At art exhibition.

Angela Davis (center) in a California courtroom with her attorneys.

At her trial, Davis stated her innocence to the courtroom. People all over the world believed her. Black writers in New York City formed a group called Black People in Defense of Angela Davis. Music was written about the injustice being done to her, to raise money for her defense. One song was "Angela" by John Lennon and Yoko Ono. Protests, demonstrations, and petitions were completed in other countries. Twenty-five hundred women stood outside the American embassy in Ceylon, now Sri Lanka, for three days in support of Angela. In Sydney, Australia, 700 women held a march. East German citizens sent 100,000 letters to the national Free Angela Committee stating their solidarity. All these people felt that Davis was unfairly charged because she was an African American and a member of the Communist Party. Davis would soon have her day in court. ■

We WANT REAL
JUSTICE
IN

END SEXUAL OPPRESION
OF WORKERS' RE

THE SOUND

SISTE
POW

SISTE
POW

HAL WAGES
PLOYMENT
ORTUNI

FREE 24-HOUR
CHILDCARE!

WOMEN'S DAY COALITION

One of many women's
rallies for equality in the
early 1970s.

2

Coming Together for Change

The Chicago Women's **Liberation** Union (CWLU) was one of the biggest and most productive organizations stemming from the women's liberation movement. On March 2, 1972, the CWLU published a pamphlet called "**Socialist** Feminism: A Strategy for the Women's Movement," circulating it nationally. The CWLU stated that gender inequality kept women down to benefit the men in power. To work on combating this injustice, the CWLU branched out into many groups.

The CWLU was organized as an umbrella organization to unite a wide range of work groups and discussion groups. One of these groups was the Chicago Women's Graphics Collective (CWGC), artists who created many of the iconic images of the women's movement. A poem titled "Mountain Moving Day" by Yosano Akiko, the pen name of a

Japanese **feminist** who lived from 1878 to 1942, was featured in a poster created by the CWGC. This poem was first published in a Japanese feminist literary magazine called *Seitō* in 1911, when it announced the beginning of the Seitōsha movement: an early Japanese women's liberation movement.

The National Black Political Convention

The National Black Political Convention took place March 10–12, 1972, at a high school in Gary, Indiana. Approximately 10,000 African Americans attended the event over the three-day period. Tensions were high because the attendees had diverse beliefs, from those who thought that working within the American political system was the most effective way to achieve their goals, to those who wanted to break away and become self-sufficient.

Reverend Jesse Jackson speaks with Coretta Scott King at the first National Black Political Convention.

Wilt Chamberlain MVP

Basketball superstar Wilt Chamberlain led the Los Angeles Lakers to win the National Basketball Association (NBA) championship over the New York Knicks on May 7, 1972.

The 7'1" power player was called the Big Dipper because of his ability to dunk a basketball straight into the hoop. The Lakers set an NBA record in the regular 1972 season by winning 33 games in a row. Chamberlain was named the championship's Most Valuable Player (MVP). This was Chamberlain's second NBA championship. He was named the NBA's season MVP four times in his career. He retired at the end of the following season after 14 years in the NBA.

Chamberlain held so many NBA records (for example, he was the only player to score 4,000 points in a season) that many people regard him as the greatest basketball player of all time.

LA Lakers Wilt Chamberlain (13) shoots the ball into the basket over NY Knicks Jerry Lucas during Game 2 of the 1972 NBA Finals.

The press interviews Jesse Jackson (center, surrounded by microphones) during the National Black Political Convention.

Elected officials mixed with Black revolutionaries in the packed high school auditorium.

The Gary Convention's goal was to create and agree upon a National Black Political Agenda that reflected the interests of African Americans. It would be used as a tool to choose their own candidates and/or endorse candidates for elective office. In this way, candidates who sought Black voters could be held accountable to Black American interests and desires. But was it possible for everyone to come together in agreement?

The convention was planned by civil rights leaders including Jesse Jackson, Amiri Baraka, Charles Diggs, Jr., Coretta Scott King, and Betty Shabazz. Jackson was an activist who had been close to Dr. King, Mrs. King was Dr. King's widow, and Shabazz was Malcolm X's widow. Baraka was a poet and recording artist. They were joined by Gary mayor Richard G. Hatcher, who was one of the first African American leaders of a large city in America.

Shirley Chisholm boycotted the event because the leaders could not decide whether to endorse her campaign in advance of the convention. This was especially painful because Diggs was her colleague in the Congressional Black Caucus.

When Jackson took the stage, he called for unity. The 1960s had delivered two major blows to African Americans: the assassinations of Malcolm X and Dr. King. The Black community had

Poet and social activist Amiri Baraka was an organizer of the National Black Political Convention.

become sharply divided on how to proceed in obtaining their civil rights. But a divided group was a diluted one. He told them that they must band together to succeed.

All the participants at the convention unified to release the Gary Declaration, detailing the crisis Black people faced in America. This declaration stated that African Americans stood united even though many of them were divided in their ideals.

The convention adapted a **preamble** to the National Black Political Agenda that declared that an effort be made to urge African Americans to view themselves as an independent force at the front of the struggle to develop a more "just and humane" society. A National Black Political Assembly was established to see that the agenda was carried out in the future.

Chisholm's Mistake

Reflecting on the convention, Baraka felt that Chisholm's decision to boycott the convention was a big mistake. Had Chisholm been there, she could have had exposure to the attendees and would have made a convincing argument as to why they should vote for her. With no candidate in attendance, the convention members voted to skip endorsing any political candidates.

Challenging School Segregation

On March 14, the NAACP filed a lawsuit against the Boston School Committee in Boston, Massachusetts. Representing 14 Black parents and 44 children, the lawsuit charged the committee with refusing to use school busing to **desegregate** their schools, even though segregation had been outlawed. The case was *Morgan v. Hennigan*. Tallulah Morgan was a 24-year-old mother of three children in the school system. James Hennigan was the chair, or head, of the Boston School Committee.

The fact that Black families and white families lived in different Boston neighborhoods kept schools segregated unless children were bused to different schools.

Students from Roxbury, Massachusetts, are bused to the Eliot School in Boston's North End during the 1971 school year.

Pop Chart Toppers

Eleven of 1972's top 20 pop songs were performed by Black artists. Roberta Flack's "The First Time Ever I Saw Your Face" was the number one song of the year. It had been featured in the soundtrack of the popular movie *Play Misty for Me*. The song spent six weeks at number one, selling over a million copies. The song won Flack a Grammy the following year, and she became the first performer to win Grammy Awards for Record of the Year two years in a row when "Killing Me Softly with His Song" won the following year.

Al Green's "Let's Stay Together" was the number one song on the 1972 soul chart and the number 11 song on the pop chart. It reached number one on the pop chart later that year as well. It was the title song on his album, which became the first of Green's six albums that would hit number one on the soul album chart.

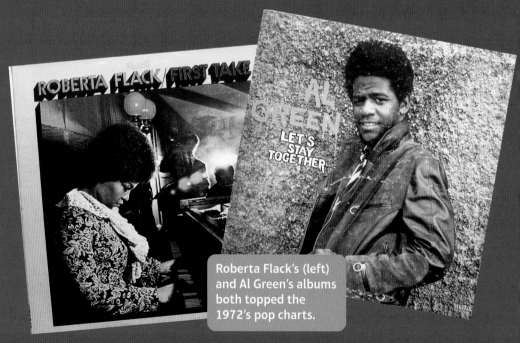

Roberta Flack's (left) and Al Green's albums both topped the 1972's pop charts.

The committee did not bus students even though there was an overcrowding issue. Rather than send white children to attend elementary schools that had been designated for Black students during segregation, the committee had portable classrooms built at the severely overcrowded formerly white schools.

Boston's secondary schools kept the racial imbalance going. Middle schools were usually in Black neighborhoods while junior highs were located in white neighborhoods. The committee converted two junior highs into middle schools, without explanation. This, the lawsuit stated, was proof that the committee wanted to keep segregation alive. The lawsuit demanded that school busing be used to **integrate** the schools. But it would be more than two years before the judge made a ruling in the case.

Shirley Chisholm said that busing students to achieve a racial balance was better than nothing, but it was an "artificial solution." She added that addressing the inequities in the housing market, which made it impossible for Black families to afford homes in certain areas, would be a real solution to creating diverse neighborhoods with diverse schools. ▪

Black Panther Party founder and Minister of Defense Huey P. Newton.

3

Equality within Reach

The Equal Rights Amendment (ERA), **legislation** that would give women equal rights and outlaw discrimination based on sex, had passed in the House of Representatives in 1970 after Shirley Chisholm gave a rousing speech. She said that there was a system of prejudice against women in America that needed to be abolished. She herself had been discriminated against far more because she was a woman than because she was Black. While prejudice against African Americans was being fought, it was still acceptable to discriminate against women, barring them from high positions and paying them less.

The ERA had stalled in the Senate that year. Senator Birch Bayh of Indiana reworded the amendment so it would be more widely accepted. He made the ERA an extension of the Fourteenth Amendment to the Constitution, which guarantees equal protection to all U.S. citizens. This new version received a much more positive response.

A Long Wait

Women had been waiting for equal rights from the U.S. government since 1923. That's when activists Alice Paul and Crystal Eastman drafted the amendment. It was introduced in Congress that year, and nearly every year afterward, and Paul had tirelessly campaigned for its passage only to see it stall in House of Representatives committees that refused to release it for a general vote. Congresswoman Martha Griffiths of Michigan found a way to bring it to the House members for a vote in 1970, and Shirley Chisholm gave it her endorsement.

Congresswoman Martha Griffiths is known as the "Mother of the ERA."

Shirley Chisholm always spoke her mind, and she was passionate about supporting the ERA.

Clear and Undeniable Need

In March 1972, the Senate Judiciary Committee reported its findings on the ERA to the full Senate. It is the committee's job to examine the need for proposed congressional legislation. The committee found that there was overwhelming evidence of continual gender discrimination in the social, cultural, and economic areas of American life. It added that the states and the courts had been too slow to address these wrongs. The report concluded that there was a "clear and undeniable need" for the ERA.

When the Senate voted on March 22, the ERA passed by the huge margin of 84 senators in favor, eight opposed. The ERA was now on its way to the states for ratification. It would need 38 states to approve it within a seven-year deadline to become a constitutional amendment.

Mexican Americans Protest Brutality

On April 9, hundreds of Mexican American youths in Santa Paula, California, began protesting police harassment and the 10 p.m. curfew that had been imposed on them. Young Mexican Americans in Ventura County, where Santa Paula was located, felt isolated in their separate neighborhoods, and they were routinely met with **racism**—including by law enforcement. No one knows what specifically triggered the Santa Paula riots but the built-up frustrations of these youths exploded. The unrest lasted until the end of April. In response to the protests, the Santa Paula Community Relations Council was created to keep communication open and problem-solve together. Mexican American youth leaders served on the council alongside city officials and police.

250 Youths Battle Santa Paula Police

SANTA PAULA, Calif. (AP) — Gunshots were fired at law enforcement officers, one car was firebombed, another auto was hit by a shotgun blast and several windows were shattered in a disturbance here involving an estimated 250 youths, police said today.

There were more than 35 arrests but no serious injuries, officers said.

Police were trying to determine today what triggered the 5-hour Sunday night disturbance.

Most of the youths were Mexican-Americans, riding in cars, and some were from Oxnard and other towns near this community 40 miles northwest of Los Angeles, police said.

Authorities said they didn't know whether the disturbance was sparked by a fight here last Friday between youths from Santa Paula and Oxnard or fueled by Mexican-Americans grievances against the police.

Officials said tension had been mounting for the past three weeks as some Mexican-Americans protested alleged "police harassment" and a 10 p.m. park curfew.

Gunfire was first reported between 7 and 7:30 p.m., and police said they called for help from nearby law enforcement agencies shortly after a shotgun blast damaged a car but caused no injuries.

About 100 law enforcement officers worked to disperse the youths. Mayor Alan Teague imposed an emergency 10 p.m. curfew.

Police said they arrested 35 to 40 persons and booked them for investigation of offenses ranging from curfew violations to arson and illegal possession of weapons.

Law enforcement officers did not return fire or use tear gas when they were met with gunfire and hurled objects, authorities said. None of the officers was injured.

Several persons, including at least one who was injured slightly when hit by shotgun pellets, were treated and released from the hospital here, officials said.

McGovern Says He'll Win Massachusetts

(Continued from Page 1)
She was all for my work, which would imply ....," she added, leaving the sentence incomplete.

Muskie's television appeals accuse President Nixon of "closed door deals" and tax giveaways. He also demanded his rivals join his call for a 90-day freeze on food prices and executive salaries.

Pennsylvania Democrats will choose among Humphrey, Muskie, McGovern, Gov. George C. Wallace of Alabama and Sen.

After the vote, Alice Paul said she had always known that equal rights were the right direction. While a lot of reforms and problems were complicated, there was nothing complicated about equality. Within two hours, the ERA had its first state ratification, from Hawaii.

Black Panther Support

On April 27, the Black Panther Party endorsed Shirley Chisholm for president. This was the first time the Panthers had aligned themselves with a political candidate. Their goal had always been to separate African Americans from the white-dominated system of society, becoming self-sufficient and self-ruling.

1972 Losses

Mahalia Jackson, a gospel singer whose hit song "Move On Up a Little Higher" sold 8 million copies and became an anthem for the budding civil rights movement in 1947, passed away on January 27 at age 60. She broke the color barrier by becoming a successful performer at a time when African Americans were segregated in large portions of the country. Jackson appeared in front of integrated crowds around the world, and she sold about 22 million records.

On October 24, Jackie Robinson, the first African American baseball player in Major League Baseball (MLB), passed away at age 53. Robinson joined the Brooklyn Dodgers in 1947 as their first baseman. He won the first Rookie of the Year award his first year in MLB. From 1949 to 1954 he was an All-Star, and in 1949 he won the National League's Most Valuable Player Award. He played in six World Series and helped the Dodgers win the World Series championship in 1955. Robinson was inducted into the Baseball Hall of Fame in 1962.

On December 3, African American jazz double bassist William Manuel "Bill" Johnson died at age 100. In the 1910s, Johnson invented the "slap" style of double bass playing when he broke his bow during

Mahalia Jackson was a friend of Dr. Martin Luther King, Jr., and his family.

a performance and started "slapping" the strings. Other musicians heard about this and tried it as well. He was the founder and manager of the Original Creole Orchestra, the first jazz band to leave New Orleans and tour widely, sharing their unique brand of jazz around the country.

On December 31, Roberto Clemente, Puerto Rican baseball right fielder for the Pittsburgh Pirates, died in a plane crash bringing emergency supplies to earthquake victims in Nicaragua. He was 38. Clemente was a two-time World Series Champion. He was an All-Star for 13 seasons and chosen for 15 All-Star Games. In 1966, he was the National League's Most Valuable Player, and he was a Gold Glove Award winner for 12 seasons straight, from 1961 through 1972. In 1973, Clemente was inducted into the Baseball Hall of Fame. He became both the first Latin American and the first Caribbean player to be honored.

After he retired from baseball, Jackie Robinson raised money for both the National Association for the Advancement of Colored People (NAACP) and the Southern Christian Leadership Conference (SCLC).

Huey P. Newton, leader of the Panthers, said that they were willing to work within the system for the good of the Black community. Gaining more control of the economic, political, and social institutions within society was the goal. He called on all Black, poor, and progressive citizens to vote for Chisholm.

The Panthers were working hard for voter registration in African American communities. In a three-day campaign the previous month, they had signed on 11,000 new voters in Oakland, California, alone.

Chisholm accepted and embraced the Black Panthers' endorsement, something many political candidates might not have done. The Panthers were controversial and targeted by the Federal Bureau of Investigation (FBI). Their meetings were frequently raided, and their members arrested. Chisholm said that the Panthers' experiences as an oppressed group in the United States—having heard empty promises from other politicians—led them to believe that she offered hope. ■

A campaign button for Shirley Chisholm's 1972 presidential candidacy.

Members of the Black Panther Party in 1971.

A 1972 San Francisco peace rally calls for the United States to leave Vietnam.

4

Spring Reckoning

Anti-war activism broke out across the country after President Nixon announced that the United States would mine, or put explosive devices, in the harbors in North Vietnam. This would prevent ships bringing supplies from docking in North Vietnam. Nixon made the announcement on May 8, to the outrage of citizens everywhere. In the previous two years, there had been fewer U.S. casualties, and the belief was that Nixon was trying to end the war. Instead, this action escalated the war against North Vietnam, and thousands of activists were dismayed and outraged.

Students made up most of the protesters, demonstrating across the country on their campuses and in the streets. Some were peaceful— mass marches, silent **vigils**, and **sit-ins** that blocked traffic—but there was also window smashing and riots. There were clashes with police who used tear gas, riot gear, sticks, police

Vietnam Veterans Against the War join other anti-war activists marching in protest near Convention Hall in Miami, Florida.

dogs, and high-pressure hoses on the students. In some cases, the school faculty and administration joined in the protesting, risking arrest.

Other citizens were moved to protest, including a group of 200 veterans called Vietnam Veterans Against the War, who tried to storm the United Nations (UN) headquarters in New York City. The UN is an organization to which most of the world's countries belong, dedicated to securing peace around the globe. Other veterans occupied the 630-foot Gateway Arch in St. Louis for two hours.

Protesters blocked the entrance to Nixon's reelection headquarters in Philadelphia, and in Washington, DC, activists shouted anti-war slogans inside the House of Representatives.

Shirley Chisholm continued to campaign hard against the war, calling for Nixon to bring the troops home. The money spent on funding those mines and the manpower required could be used to "revitalize and rebuild our cities," she said.

Continued Discrimination

Vietnam was the first American war fought with desegregated troops. Black soldiers had been treated horribly while segregated. They

BLACK PEOPLE: 10% IN U. S. 22% IN VIETNAM
W H Y ?

A protest button questions the high rate at which African Americans were drafted into the Vietnam War.

Black and white U.S. Marines march in step with one another in Vietnam.

received lower ranks, lower salaries, and the most dangerous assignments. Their risk of death was greater because they had inadequate training and not enough weapons and equipment.

Despite desegregation, African American soldiers were still met with racism and inequities. They were sent to the front lines in greater numbers than white soldiers, disciplined more often, and promoted less. While they fought side by side with white soldiers in battle, back at the bases, the men remained separate.

Sentences Overturned

On May 11, a Chicago court of appeals set aside the severe sentences for **contempt of court** that had been handed to the Chicago Eight—Bobby Seale, Black Panther Party leader, and the seven other defendants who had stood trial for conspiracy to **incite** riots at the 1968 Democratic National Convention—plus their two lawyers. The contempt charges were overturned, but not dismissed, and sent to a new judge for review.

During the trial, Seale had been sentenced to four years in prison for protesting that his lawyer was not present (he was in the hospital) and that he was not allowed to represent himself.

Portraits of the Chicago Eight; Bobby Seale is pictured bottom left.

Death of J. Edgar Hoover

On May 2, the director of the FBI, J. Edgar Hoover, died. He had run the FBI for nearly five decades, abusing the agency's power by **persecuting** anyone he believed to be a threat against the country. He began a secret and illegal counterintelligence program called COINTELPRO in 1956, expanding it to gather massive files on anyone he labeled as **radical**. Hate groups like the Ku Klux Klan (KKK) were infiltrated, but so were African American civil rights organizations and anti-war groups. Dr. King was a COINTELPRO target and was continually harassed by the FBI. Congress suspected the FBI of criminal activity. When Hoover died, the agency was investigated, and Hoover's decades of discriminatory acts came to light.

J. Edgar Hoover served as director of the FBI from 1924 to 1972.

Bobby Seale (left) and his lawyer, Charles Garry, in the San Francisco City Jail before Seale was transported to Chicago for trial.

Judge Julius Hoffman not only cited Seale for contempt multiple times, but he also ordered Seale be bound and gagged while in the courtroom—an injustice that went on for several days before Seale was granted a **mistrial**. His case was separated from the rest of the defendants. Eventually, the charges against Seale for conspiracy were dropped, but the contempt charges—and the four-year sentence—had remained.

The other defendants were all **acquitted** of conspiracy, but five of them were convicted of crossing state lines to incite a riot. They were each sentenced to five years in jail and given a $5,000 fine. Those convictions were appealed.

The appeal judges ruled that Hoffman had abused his power by dismissing Bobby Seale's protests that he lacked legal representation.

Backfire

The case against the Chicago Eight had been unjust from the beginning. These eight men had all been targeted by the FBI and the Nixon administration as threats. They had publicly spoken out against unjust

Nixon (left) and Hoover in Washington, DC, in 1969.

THE CONSPIRACY EIGHT GETTING READY FOR CHICAGO TRIAL

CHICAGO (LNS) -- The coercive machinery of nationwide political repression is high-powered and well-tooled. The use of laws which blatantly restrict the basic precepts of Constitutional democracy -- the abstract freedoms of speech, press and assembly -- is constantly growing.

While a frame-up on non-political charges (from possession of marijuana to trespassing) is still the most frequent form of repression, the government is now turning to more direct methods of silencing its opposition.

The anti-riot section of the 1968 Civil Rights Act permits the federal government to throw any radical or movement organizer into jail for five years if he so much as discusses a planned demonstration or rally with two or more people.

In its first run, the government is trying to pin the responsibility for the police riot in Chicago during last August's Democratic Convention on

The chief promoters of the Yippie media myth, Abbie Hoffman and Jerry Rubin, are perhaps more glamorous defendants than the Mobe organizers. Abbie and Jerry are the personification of everything Chicago's Mayor Daley finds disgusting. They devote most of their energies to no-holds-barred spur-of-the-moment theater -- street theater in the streets and theater of the absurd in Congressional committee meetings -- a tactic which obviously disturbs the government even though it does not involve a disciplined revolutionary organization.

John Froines and Lee Weiner are university radicals. John is an assistant and professor of chemistry at the University of Oregon and Lee is a research assistant at Northwestern University in Chicago. While the government's attack on Froines and Weiner is somewhat mysterious because they are so much more obscure than the other defendants, certainly the most amazing indictment is that of Black Panther Party Chairman

mascot. Judge Magoo is 74 years old and many Conspiracy staff members are making bets that he won't live past the trial. His wife is a major stock-holder in a corporation which makes gadgets for the Vietnam war, and, not surprisingly, he has a record of giving draft resisters and other "subversives" the harshest penalties permitted by law.

After three costly delays, Magoo decided not to rule on a defense motion for the release of illegal wire-tap records the government readily admits to having. The reason? The motion was of such a heavy nature that Magoo felt he could not possibly rule on it until after the trial was over. Conspirator Abbie Hoffman retaliated with a claim that he is Judge Hoffman's illegitimate nephew, but Magoo was unmoved.

Another figure in the kangaroo court is the prosecutor, U.S. District Attorney Thomas Foran, a Democrat who suddenly started working to build a go-getter, gang-buster image

again in the govern... ... ... crush the p... mond J... Righ... g...

boo.

Anot.

Mitchell's ... the government ... Long Amendment to the same act. This amendment -- Louisiana Senator Russell Long's contribution to the jurisprudence of repression -- makes it a felony to make any effort to get in the way of any cop who is going about his "business." Combine that one with the conspiracy laws

A headline from *The Black Panther* newspaper in 1969.

government policies surrounding the Vietnam War and police brutality. It was clear that the charges were not true—some of these men had never met before the convention, let alone planned a riot together. Bobby Seale had not even been scheduled to appear.

The previous presidential administration had declined to press charges. But when Nixon took office in 1969, he and FBI director J. Edgar Hoover decided to have the eight men arrested and tried as an attempt to silence the peace movement against the war in Vietnam—and the Black Power movement. Both were threats to the administration because they were so vocal in their criticisms and rallied people to protest.

But the plan to silence the Chicago Eight backfired against the government. The case became a media sensation and only served to raise more protest and outrage against oppression.

Seale for Mayor

Bobby Seale announced his candidacy for mayor of Oakland, California, on May 13. Campaigning for Shirley Chisholm had thrust him into politics, instead of fighting the system like he'd done previously, and he realized he could help Black citizens if he was an elected official. He was already getting voters registered by the thousands for Chisholm, so it was perfect timing for more exposure and to discuss the issues

A campaign car used to spread the word about Bobby Seale's mayoral candidacy in Oakland, California.

VOTE APRIL 17TH *Elect* **BOBBY SEALE** A DEMOCRAT MAYOR OF OAKLAND

he was running his campaign on: allowing community control of the police and putting a limit on how high rent could be. The election would take place the following year.

Humanity above Politics

On May 15, a day before the Maryland Democratic primary, George Wallace was shot at his campaign stop in Laurel, Maryland. After a well-received speech, he exited the stage and began shaking hands with people when shots rang from the crowd. Several other people were shot as well before another member of the crowd took the shooter, Arthur Bremer, down.

In 1963, Alabama governor George Wallace stands in the door of the all-white University of Alabama to block the end of segregation.

Wallace, shot five times and critically injured, was rushed to the hospital.

When Shirley Chisholm heard the news, she was overcome with concern and compassion for Wallace. He had been threatened with assassination, and she realized that it could have been her just as easily as it had been Wallace. Even more than that, she cared that a human being was suffering.

Chisholm went to Holy Cross Hospital in Silver Spring to see Wallace. Holding his hand, she told him that she wouldn't want what happened to him to happen to anyone. She also told him that although they disagreed profoundly about civil rights issues, she agreed with his views that corporations should not be allowed to dominate the country and the fact that the government had been unresponsive to the people.

Indian Education Act of 1972

On June 23, Congress passed the landmark Indian Education Act. This act authorized additional funding to school districts where many American Indian and Alaska Native children attended. This historic legislation established a new and complete way of meeting the culturally related academic needs of these students, and it acknowledged the federal government's responsibility. The act covered preschool to graduate-level education. It provided services that the Bureau of Indian Affairs (BIA)—the federal agency responsible for administering to the care of Indigenous Americans—did not.

Navajo children learn arithmetic at a government-run school on their reservation.

Shirley Chisholm tells reporters she had a very pleasant visit with George Wallace in the hospital.

After 15 minutes, doctors told Chisholm that she must leave. Wallace was in grave condition. He gripped her hand tightly, not wanting her to go.

Receiving criticism for visiting Wallace, Chisholm made no apologies. She said that the visit was the humane thing to do. Politics could not be allowed to make one forget they were a human being.

Unity Dissolves

On May 19, the leaders of the National Black Political Convention released the National Black Political Agenda as guidelines for Black political activity. These guidelines had been voted on and agreed to in Gary, Indiana—but things had changed.

In the two months since the convention, the unity that had been achieved had begun to erode. Many convention members were rethinking their agreement to work with other African Americans who held different beliefs than their own.

The NAACP was one of several Black organizations that withdrew support of the agenda. This ended the harmony and unity that had been achieved. The Black Power movement was especially hurt, because it did not have the political power that the more mainstream groups did.

On behalf of the convention's organizers, Amiri Baraka said that no matter what the convention attendees' differences were, they would not give up trying to achieve political unity among African American activists and elected officials. ◼

Black National Convention programs lay on seats at West Side High School in Gary, Indiana, on March 11, 1972.

A jubilant Angela Davis celebrates her acquittal alongside Franklin Alexander (right), leader of the Angela Davis Defense Committee.

5

A Hot Time

An all-white jury in San Jose, California, found Angela Davis not guilty of murder, kidnapping, and conspiracy on June 4. After deliberating for 13 hours, jury members decided that the fact that Davis owned the guns was not enough evidence to prove she was involved in the plot to take over the courtroom.

Davis's attorney Leo Branton, Jr., had hired psychologists to observe the jury pool when jurors were being selected, to predict who would be more likely to sympathize with the defense's arguments. During the trial, he brought in experts to cast doubt on the eyewitness accounts that were offered in testimony. Branton's techniques were groundbreaking and paved the way for future trial tactics.

Shirley Chisholm gets a seat at the *Meet the Press* table after she wins her lawsuit charging that the media was ignoring her.

A Seat at the Table

One of Shirley Chisholm's most famous quotes is "If they don't give you a seat at the table, bring a folding chair." In June 1972, she sued the Federal Communications Commission (FCC), which governed broadcast communications, to be included in the Democratic presidential candidate debate.

Chisholm's lawsuit stated that the media was ignoring her campaign and failing to report on her. Specifically, she had not been invited to the first three debates. She was not invited to be part of the fourth debate in June, either, but on June 5, a court of appeals ordered her to be included. In carrying out the court's decision, the FCC ordered all broadcasters to include Chisholm in their coverage. She became the first woman to be included in a presidential debate.

Feminist Magazine

On July 1, the first issue of *Ms.* magazine was published. Dorothy Pitman Hughes, a feminist and African American activist, cofounded the magazine devoted to women's liberation. At the time, it was a bold decision for Hughes to team with Gloria Steinem, a journalist who had become a leader of the feminist movement. Hughes worried about people in her home-town of Lumpkin, Georgia, seeing her beside a white woman. But she knew she needed to do this.

The two women met in the late 1960s when Steinem interviewed Hughes for *New York Magazine*, where Steinem was a columnist. Hughes had put together a multiracial cooperative day care center in New York City, the West 80th Street Day Care and Community Center. The women became friends, and Steinem invited Hughes to join her in speaking with audiences about the women's movement. Hughes accepted the invitation. They traveled for two years and were so well received that Hughes came up with the idea of a women-operated, women-focused maga-zine. *Ms.* magazine evolved from this brainstorm.

Hughes and Steinem posed for a photo showing their feminist solidarity, raising their fists in a salute made popular in the Black Power movement.

The preview issue was published in December 1971. The cover depicted the Hindu goddess Kali pregnant, with each of her eight arms holding an object: a skillet, rake, typewriter, telephone, iron, clock, steering wheel, and mirror. This picture was called "The Housewife's Moment of Truth."

The July 1972 cover featured Wonder Woman, with the caption "Wonder Woman for President." The idea was to turn Wonder Woman into a feminist hero. Wonder Woman's powers had been taken

Published in *Esquire* magazine in October 1971, this photo of Gloria Steinem (left) and Dorothy Pitman Hughes becomes a symbol of feminist solidarity.

George McGovern (center) celebrates his Democratic nomination for president with a group of Black leaders.

George McGovern of South Dakota. McGovern had gathered 1,729 delegates in the primaries, and he did not need to negotiate anything to secure the nomination.

The important thing about the convention was to not only choose the candidate—as he had in effect already been chosen—but to establish that the whole party was behind him. Party unity was vital to succeed in the general election against Nixon. Even Congressman Ronald V. Dellums, Chisholm's strongest supporter at the convention and her old friend who had started the Congressional Black Caucus with her, told her he had to support McGovern. Now, he said, they had to be realistic and do what was best for the party.

First Female FBI Agents

J. Edgar Hoover had not allowed women to become special agents in the FBI. His rule was banished shortly after he died, and two women joined 43 men for training at the FBI headquarters in Quantico, Virginia, in July 1972.

Joanne Pierce Misko, 31, who had been a nun for 10 years previously, and Susan Roley Malone, 25, who had been a U.S. Marine, needed to meet the same physical requirements as the men—and they did.

Once they'd completed their training, they were sent to posts in Omaha, Nebraska, and St. Louis, Missouri. After they proved they could handle themselves, they were accepted by their male coworkers. The women never wanted any special treatment or publicity—they only wanted to be special agents.

Joanne Pierce Misko (center) was one of two women sworn in as FBI special agents in 1972.

Congressman Ronald V. Dellums.

Before Chisholm's delegates left the floor—they could no longer stay there once McGovern claimed the nomination—she gave a unity speech. She told her supporters, "We gained experience." Chisholm ended her campaign without achieving her goals at the convention, but she was proud to have set the stage for future diverse candidates. She had stepped up and set out for the impossible, and she had spoken her mind. Truly, she was unbought and unbossed. She later said that she wanted to be remembered as having guts. ■

An Indigenous American woman stands wrapped in an upside-down American flag at the Bureau of Indian Affairs in Washington, DC.

6

Broken Promises

In October 1972, eight members of the First Nation organization set out in a caravan of buses, cars, trucks, and campers across the country, in protest of the lies and betrayal they had received from the U.S. government and to receive justice. Stretching over four miles long, the caravan left from St. Paul, Minnesota, with the Bureau of Indian Affairs (BIA) in Washington, DC, as their destination. Filled with corruption and scandal, the BIA had mishandled Indian affairs, hurting the people they were supposed to help.

Before leaving, activists worked together to develop the 20-Point Position Paper, which stated the demands that they were delivering for negotiation. Hank Adams, an Assiniboine activist who had traveled from Washington State, wrote the draft. They expected to meet with President Nixon.

Many of the points addressed the Indigenous Americans' desire to be self-governing and to be able to renegotiate treaties. But some of them were about necessities. One of the points was the critical need for sanitary sewers and clean drinking water on reservations. Indigenous American children were dying from environmentally induced diseases due to broken heating systems and contaminated water sources. The paper pointed out that in recent years more government money had

American artist Max D. Standley's oil painting *Trail of Tears* depicts the suffering the Cherokee people endured when they were forcibly removed from their land.

been spent on hotel bills for Indigenous American—related problem-solving meetings, conferences, and conventions than what had been spent on necessary reservation housing.

Trail of Tears

The Indigenous Americans called their caravan the Trail of Broken Treaties, a reference to the Trail of Tears—the forced displacement of approximately 60,000 Indigenous Americans from their homes and land beginning in 1830. It was 5,043 miles long and covered nine states: Alabama, Arkansas,

Georgia, Illinois, Kentucky, Missouri, North Carolina, Oklahoma, and Tennessee. Many thousands of people did not survive the journey, dying from disease and starvation. The young and the elderly were particularly vulnerable. Those who made it were promised that their new land would always be Native territory, but by 1907, all of that land had been turned into U.S. states.

Occupying the BIA

The caravan had between 700 and 1,000 activists representing more than 200 tribes from 25 states. It gained attention along the way to

A tepee set up outside the Bureau of Indian Affairs in protest of the government's treatment of Indigenous Americans.

Indigenous Americans display an upside-down American flag on the steps of the Bureau of Indian Affairs on November 6, five days after their occupation of the building began.

Washington, DC. The Indigenous people they encountered felt empowered to see this activism.

But on November 2, things went wrong at the BIA. First, Nixon sent word that he refused to meet with the members of the caravan. Then, as the protesting Indigenous Americans negotiated for their housing, BIA guards mistakenly tried to physically remove several Native youth from the building because it was after hours. These youth overpowered the guards and threw them out of the building. The activists broke up furniture from all over the building to barricade the entrances and use as weapons. An occupation was happening.

Nixon tended to respond to threats of violence with a return of violence. When no offer for

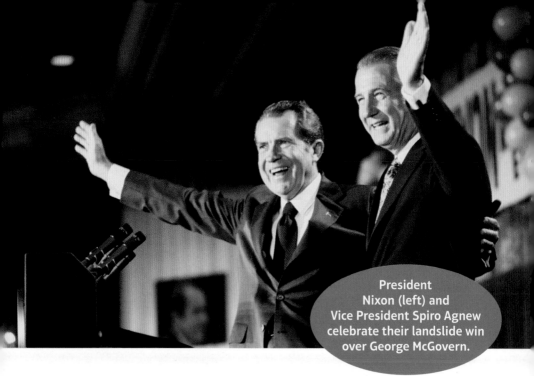

President Nixon (left) and Vice President Spiro Agnew celebrate their landslide win over George McGovern.

negotiation came, the activists realized that they had put themselves in an extremely dangerous situation. They put out a call for help through the media, and hundreds of local citizens blocked the building's entrances with their bodies.

The presidential election was about to happen on November 7, and Nixon did not want any negative attention until it was over. A deadline was set for the Indigenous Americans to surrender; it was ignored. This happened several times. Undercover agents spied on the area, army trucks pulled up in front of the building, and police patrol cars circled it. But the activists would not be intimidated. Some donned war paint, which symbolized that they would fight to the death.

Agreement Reached

Nixon defeated George McGovern in a landslide. Once victory was secured, the government appointed a negotiator, who met with Hank Adams. Adams was able to negotiate a promise from Nixon's administration that the Indigenous occupiers would not be prosecuted. It was agreed that the BIA would appoint an Indigenous American to a position in their office. And the federal government agreed to more treaty negotiations.

Indigenous Americans reach the Capitol after completing a 2,800-mile trek that started five months earlier in California.

The occupation ended on November 8. Upon leaving the building, the activists took Native artwork and artifacts with them. No one attempted to stop them.

The government broke a promise when it later prosecuted occupiers for $2 million in damages to the building. The government claimed this had not been included in their agreement.

A Step toward Sovereignty

The 20 points largely remained unaddressed. But the Trail of Broken Treaties brought the ongoing disgraceful treatment of Indigenous Americans into public awareness. Hank Adams and other activists used this momentum to plan future demonstrations. Most importantly, the Trail of Broken Treaties built support for Indigenous **sovereignty**. It raised Indigenous peoples' determination to be self-governing and work together for their rights.

Black Representatives

On November 7, Barbara Jordan and Andrew Young were elected to the U.S. House of Representatives, becoming the first African American representatives from southern states since 1898.

Jordan had run in 1962 and 1964 for the Texas House of Representatives, losing both times. In 1966, she ran for the Texas Senate and won, becoming the

first Black state senator in the United States since 1883. Her 30 senate colleagues, all white males, didn't welcome her warmly, but she won them over by being an effective legislator. In 1972, they elected her as the leader of the state senate, and she became the first African American woman in America to head a legislative body. One of her duties in that job was to act as governor when both the governor and the lieutenant governor were out of state. She did this on June 10, 1972—making her the first Black chief executive in the country.

Andrew Young had been Dr. King's senior aide in the Southern Christian Leadership Conference (SCLC) in the 1960s. King had relied on him, especially when King and Reverend Ralph Abernathy, King's chief aide, were arrested and incarcerated for training students to register voters.

Black Girl

Black Girl, a film exploring the experiences and issues Black women faced in the 1970s, was released on November 9. Based on a 1969 play, it also addressed the stereotypes Black women faced at that time and their specific issues within the feminist movement.

The story follows a single Black woman who struggles to take care of her family but refuses to let her ex-husband save her. It deals with her relationship with her daughters as well.

This movie showed that roles for Black women were expanding and no longer stereotypical. It was time to examine the struggles that these women faced and to show that they had relevant stories to share.

A poster for the film *Black Girl*.

Andrew Young (left) accompanies Dr. King at a 1967 Chicago press conference.

King named Young executive director of the SCLC in 1964, and Young was instrumental in providing support for demonstrations and legislation such as the landmark Civil Rights Act of 1964 and the Voting Rights Act of 1965. He resigned in 1970 to pursue politics, running to represent Georgia in the House of Representatives. He continued to believe in **nonviolent resistance**, and he planned to bring King's beliefs for civil rights to the forefront of the nation once more.

Freedom of Speech Upheld

On November 21, all the convictions of the Chicago Seven—formerly the Chicago Eight—were dismissed by a United States Court of Appeals. The judges found Judge Hoffman's actions were grounds for reversal, as were the actions of the prosecution. It had come out that the prosecution and the FBI had planted listening devices in the defense attorneys' offices. In July, a judge had declined Bobby Seale's contempt of court charges, and the courts also declined to retry him on the original charges of conspiring to incite a riot and crossing state lines to do so. One of the judges filed a separate opinion that the Anti-Riot Act, which had been used to charge the eight men, **unconstitutionally** infringed on their freedom of speech.

With J. Edgar Hoover dead and Richard Nixon in the midst of Watergate, a scandal that would lead to his resignation, this condemnation of what had been done to the Chicago Eight was clearance for civil rights activists to further speak their minds. ▪

Death of Harry S. Truman

Former president Harry S. Truman died at age 88 on December 26, 1972. He had been vice president to Franklin D. Roosevelt and thrust unexpectedly into the presidency when Roosevelt died in 1945.

Growing up in Missouri, Truman had been instilled with racism. Civil rights leaders worried about the harm he would cause their mission—and certainly they never imagined he would help it. But when Truman, a veteran himself, learned about Isaac Woodard, a Black veteran savagely beaten and blinded by South Carolina police, he responded.

After Truman received a report detailing the horrors that African Americans were enduring in the United States, he went into action, tasking Congress to pass civil rights legislation. Unfortunately, Congress was not on board no matter how much he called them out. But Truman did what his authority allowed: In 1948, he signed Executive Order 9981, which ended racial segregation in the armed forces. Truman's devotion to civil rights nearly cost him reelection—but he won thanks to the support of African American voters.

President Truman became a huge supporter of civil rights during his terms.

Vice President Kamala Harris said, "We stand on the shoulders of Shirley Chisholm and Shirley Chisholm stood proud."

The Legacy of 1972 in Civil Rights History

Shirley Chisholm wrote a book about her experiences running for president. In *The Good Fight*, she made it clear that she had run with the intention of paving the way for someone else to succeed. She wrote, "because somebody had to do it first."

Senator Kamala Harris of California ran for the Democratic nomination for president in the 2020 election. She did not win the nomination, but Joe Biden, who did win, selected her as his running mate. When they won the election, Harris became the first woman vice president, the first African American vice president, and the first Asian American vice president. Harris said that Shirley Chisholm paved the way for her victory.

Paralyzed from the waist down, George Wallace never forgot Shirley Chisholm's visit to him in the hospital. Several years later, Chisholm was working on a bill to give domestic workers the right to a minimum wage. Wallace convinced enough of the southern congressmen to vote for the bill and the legislation passed through the House.

Bobby Seale received the second most votes for mayor of Oakland, California, in 1973, out of nine candidates. He lost a runoff, or tie breaker, election against sitting mayor John Reading, but he proved how powerful his voice had become.

Angela Davis's experiences in the U.S. prison system inspired her to fight against the nation's political interests that encourage spending money on imprisonment, even when it isn't justified.

The National Black Political Assembly, which had been created at the National Black Political

A 2020 Black Lives Matter demonstration in New York's Times Square draws thousands seeking equality and justice for Black Americans.

Convention, fell apart due to the group's conflicting ideas and ideals. Two more conventions were held in later years, but they were much less advertised and not well attended. Despite this, the legacy of the National Black Political Convention has remained.

Black Lives Matter (BLM), a political and social movement, was created in 2013 to highlight racism, discrimination, and inequality experienced by Black Americans. The movement was inspired to use the Gary Convention as a model for uniting their ideas and energy and shifting it into political empowerment. BLM is now a global organization that fights for "Freedom, Liberation, and Justice" for the Black community. ■

Kristen Clarke

Kristen Clarke during her April 14, 2021, hearing to be confirmed Assistant Attorney General, Civil Rights Division at the Department of Justice, in Washington, DC.

Kristen Clarke has devoted her life to bringing equal justice to all American citizens. She started her career at the U.S. Department of Justice Civil Rights Division, where she worked as a trial attorney prosecuting hate crimes and other civil rights violations. Twenty-one years later, she returned to the U.S. Department of Justice Civil Rights Division. President Joe Biden appointed her Assistant Attorney General for Civil Rights in 2021, and she made history by becoming the first woman to be responsible for carrying out the division's mission to enforce civil rights laws and ensure that all American citizens are guaranteed their civil and constitutional rights.

Raised in Brooklyn, New York, by parents who were Jamaican immigrants, Clarke was raised to appreciate every opportunity and to work hard in school. She was a member of Prep for Prep, a program that helps gifted and high-achieving students of color attend private schools. She attended Choate Rosemary Hall, a private college preparatory school in Connecticut, and afterward attended Harvard University. She then went to Columbia Law School and earned her juris doctor degree.

After prosecuting federal civil rights cases for six years, Clarke joined the NAACP

Kristen Clarke's official portrait as assistant attorney general.

Shelby County v. Holder before the Supreme Court, attempting to gain access to voting for Black citizens of Shelby County, Alabama. Unfortunately, the Supreme Court ruled against the reform. Disappointment is a part of every civil rights attorney's career, but Clarke did not let her loss get in the way of her determination to bring equal rights to everyone.

Legal Defense Fund. Clarke co-led the political participation group, which worked on voting rights for Black Americans and election law reform. She argued the case

Clarke was appointed director of the civil rights bureau of the Attorney General of New York's office in 2011. She worked

"Our nation is a healthier place when we respect the rights of all communities."

—KRISTEN CLARKE

On May 25, 2021, Vice President Kamala Harris (right) swears in Kristen Clarke (left) as assistant attorney general. Clarke's mother, Pansy Clarke, holds the Bible.

to eliminate racial profiling in retail stores and consulted police departments about reforming their profiling policies. She also focused on housing discrimination.

In 2015, Clarke joined the Lawyers' Committee for Civil Rights Under Law, a civil rights organization that consists of private practice lawyers working to enforce civil rights for all. Clarke continued her devotion to voter rights by championing the John Lewis Voting Rights Advancement Act, which would restore strengths of the Voting Rights Act of 1965 that had been lost. In 2020, Clarke sued the United States Postal Service for its failure to send out voting ballots for the presidential election in a timely fashion during the pandemic.

The recipient of numerous awards and distinctions, Clarke set out on her path to protect the civil rights of all American citizens at the

Kristen Clarke speaks at The Queen theater in Wilmington, Delaware, on January 7, 2021.

start of her career, and she never veered from it. The *New York Times* called her one of the nation's biggest champions of voting rights, and President Joe Biden put the trust of the country in her hands. Her responsibility, he said, was to guarantee justice to the people of this nation. Clarke welcomed this enormous undertaking— her opportunity to achieve the goal she had always carried in her heart. ■

TIMELINE

The Year in Civil Rights

1972

MARCH 2

The CWLU publishes a pamphlet called "Socialist Feminism: A Strategy for the Women's Movement," circulating it nationally.

JANUARY 25

Congresswoman Shirley Chisholm announces her candidacy for the Democratic Party's presidential nomination.

MARCH 22

The Senate votes and passes the Equal Rights Amendment by a huge margin of 84 senators in favor, eight opposed.

FEBRUARY

Representative Ronald V. Dellums of California introduces the Congressional Black Caucus's first bill concerning apartheid into Congress.

APRIL 9

Hundreds of Mexican American youths in Santa Paula, California, begin protesting police harassment.

250 Youths Battle Santa Paula Police

MAY 7

Basketball superstar Wilt Chamberlain leads the Los Angeles Lakers to win the National Basketball Association championship over the New York Knicks.

MAY 13

Bobby Seale announces his candidacy for mayor of Oakland, California.

JUNE 23

Congress passes the landmark Indian Education Act.

JULY 1

The first issue of *Ms.* magazine, cofounded by Dorothy Pitman Hughes and Gloria Steinem, is published.

OCTOBER 24

Jackie Robinson, the first African American player in Major League Baseball, passes away at age 53.

NOVEMBER 7

Barbara Jordan and Andrew Young are elected to the House of Representatives, becoming the first African American representatives from southern states since 1898.

DECEMBER 26

Former president Harry S. Truman dies at the age of 88.

GLOSSARY

abolish (uh-BAH-lish) to put an end to something officially

acquit (uh-KWIT) to find someone not guilty of a crime

activist (AK-tuh-vist) a person who works to bring about political or social change

amendment (uh-MEND-muhnt) a change that is made to a law or a legal document

apartheid (uh-PAHR-tide) in South Africa, a policy and system of segregation and discrimination on the basis of race

boycott (BOI-kaht) a refusal to buy something or do business with someone as a protest

civil rights (SIV-uhl rites) the individual rights that all members of a democratic society have to freedom and equal treatment under the law

Communist (KAHM-yuh-nist) an advocate of communism, which is a system in which goods are owned in common and are available to all as needed

conspiracy (kuhn-SPEER-uh-see) a secret plan made by two or more people to do something illegal or harmful

contempt of court (kuhn-TEMPT uhv kort) open disrespect of the orders, authority, or dignity of a court or judge acting in a judicial capacity by disruptive language or conduct or by failure to obey the court's orders

delegate (DEL-i-git) someone who represents other people at a meeting or in a legislature

desegregate (dee-SEG-ruh-gate) to do away with the practice of separating people of different races in schools, restaurants, and other public places

discrimination (dis-krim-uh-NAY-shuhn) prejudice or unfair behavior to others based on differences in such things as race, gender, or age

domestic (duh-MES-tik) of or having to do with the home

economic (ek-uh-NAH-mik) of or having to do with the way money, resources, and services are used in a society

federal (FED-ur-uhl) having to do with the national government, as opposed to state or local government

feminist (FEM-uh-nist) someone who believes strongly that women are equal to men and should have the same rights and opportunities

incite (in-SITE) to stir up feelings that make someone do something violent or foolish

indigenous (in-DI-juh-nuhs) produced, living, or existing naturally in a particular region or environment

integrate (IN-ti-grate) to make facilities or an organization open to people of all races and ethnic groups

Jim Crow (jim kro) the former practice of segregating Black people in the United States

legislation (lej-is-LAY-shuhn) a law or set of laws that have been proposed or made

liberation (lib-uh-RAY-shuhn) the act of freeing someone or something from imprisonment, slavery, or oppression

lynching (LIN-ching) a sometimes public murder by a group of people, often involving hanging

mistrial (MIS-trye-uhl) a trial that has no legal effect with regard to one or more of the charges brought against the defendant because of some serious error or misconduct in the proceedings or a hung jury

nonviolent resistance (nahn-VYE-uh-luhnt ri-ZIS-tuhns) peaceful demonstration for political purpose

oppress (uh-PRES) to use power or authority in a cruel and unfair way

persecute (PUR-suh-kyoot) to cause to suffer because of belief

preamble (pree-AM-buhl) an introductory statement

prejudice (PREJ-uh-dis) immovable, unreasonable, or unfair opinion about someone based on the person's race, religion, or other characteristic

racism (RAY-si-zuhm) thinking that a particular race is better than others or treating people unfairly or cruelly because of their race

radical (RAD-i-kuhl) associated with political views, practices, and policies of extreme change

segregation (seg-ruh-GAY-shuhn) the act or practice of keeping people or groups apart

sit-in (SIT-in) a form of protest in which demonstrators occupy a place, refusing to leave until their demands are met

Socialist (SOH-shuh-list) one who advocates or practices socialism; any of various economic and political theories advocating collective or governmental ownership and administration of goods and services

sovereignty (SAHV-rin-tee) supreme authority or the power to rule

unconstitutional (uhn-kahn-sti-TOO-shuh-nuhl) not in keeping with the basic principles or laws set forth in the U.S. Constitution

vigil (VIJ-uhl) an event or a period of time when a person or group stays in a place and quietly waits, prays, etc., especially at night

BIBLIOGRAPHY

Aronson, Marc. *Master of Deceit: J. Edgar Hoover and America in the Age of Lies.* Somerville, MA: Candlewick Press, 2012.

Chisholm, Shirley. *The Good Fight.* New York: Amistad, 2022. First published 1973 by HarperCollins.

Farrell, Amy Erdman. *Yours in Sisterhood: Ms. Magazine and the Promise of Popular Feminism.* Chapel Hill, NC: The University of North Carolina Press, 1998.

Lynch, Shola, dir. *Chisholm '72: Unbought and Unbossed.* 2004.

Moore, Leonard N. *The Defeat of Black Power: Civil Rights and the National Black Political Convention of 1972.* Baton Rouge, LA: LSU Press, 2018.

Wallace, Terry. *Bloods: Black Veterans of the Vietnam War: An Oral History.* Novato, CA: Presidio Press, 1985.

Shirley Chisholm and her campaign workers flash the victory sign after she is elected to represent New York City's Bedford-Stuyvesant neighborhood in Congress on November 5, 1968.

INDEX

About the Author

Selene Castrovilla is an acclaimed, award-winning author. Her five books on the American Revolution for young readers include Scholastic's *The Founding Mothers*. Selene has been a meticulous researcher of American history since 2003. She has expanded her exploration into the civil rights movement, as well as the Civil War, in a forthcoming book. A frequent speaker about our nation's evolution, she is equally comfortable with audiences of children and adults. Please visit selenecastrovilla.com.

PHOTO CREDITS